THE LULLABY

A Play in One Act for Four Women

by

MICHAEL DINES

SAMUEL  FRENCH

LONDON
NEW YORK TORONTO SYDNEY · HOLLYWOOD

Copyright © 1960 by Samuel French Ltd
All Rights Reserved

THE LULLABY is fully protected under the copyright laws of the British Commonwealth, including Canada, the United States of America, and all other countries of the Copyright Union. All rights, including professional and amateur stage productions, recitation, lecturing, public reading, motion picture, radio broadcasting, television and the rights of translation into foreign languages are strictly reserved.

ISBN 978-0-573-03270-7

www.samuelfrench.co.uk
www.samuelfrench.com

FOR AMATEUR PRODUCTION ENQUIRIES

UNITED KINGDOM AND WORLD EXCLUDING NORTH AMERICA
plays@SamuelFrench-London.co.uk
020 7255 4302/01

Each title is subject to availability from Samuel French, depending upon country of performance.

CAUTION: Professional and amateur producers are hereby warned that THE LULLABY is subject to a licensing fee. Publication of this play does not imply availability for performance. Both amateurs and professionals considering a production are strongly advised to apply to the appropriate agent before starting rehearsals, advertising, or booking a theatre. A licensing fee must be paid whether the title is presented for charity or gain and whether or not admission is charged.

The professional rights in this play are controlled by Samuel French Ltd, 52 Fitzroy Street, London, W1T 5JR.

No one shall make any changes in this title for the purpose of production. No part of this book may be reproduced, stored in a retrieval system, or transmitted in any form, by any means, now known or yet to be invented, including mechanical, electronic, photocopying, recording, videotaping, or otherwise, without the prior written permission of the publisher. No one shall upload this title, or part of this title, to any social media websites.

The right of Michael Dines to be identified as author of this work has been asserted in accordance with Section 77 of the Copyright, Designs and Patents Act 1988.

AUTHOR'S NOTE

The Lullaby is a play of four women. It is based on a real-life occurrence with allowance for dramatic licence.

The MOTHER SUPERIOR and SISTER THÉRÈSE are two women of gentle disposition and if at times SISTER THÉRÈSE tries to be strict, her attempt is not very successful.

The two nuns wear the usual religious habit: black veil and robes, white coif, flat shoes and black stockings.

MADAME LATTIER is the typical Gallic peasant—of the earth, indestructible. She wears a voluminous skirt, blouse, heavy and serviceable shoes or boots. Her clothing, while plain, is obviously her best. The bag she carries is of fabric or cloth, a type of large hold-all, and is about twenty-four inches by eighteen in size.

MARIE is a child with a dim remembrance of the tragedy behind her, a mixture of hope and shyness. Her difficulty in speaking is more pronounced at some times than others, but at all times this must not be exaggerated. I have given an approximate age for this character, but in case of difficulty in casting, this age can be altered by a few years either way.

A suitable piece of music for the lullaby is *Chanson Pour une Poupée* by Kosma Bassis, but should any difficulty be met in obtaining it, there are many similar songs that would do—any reasonable folk-song or lullaby. It can be sung or hummed according to the musical capabilities of the cast. The song chosen should also be used for opening and closing the play.

THE LULLABY

Presented at the College of Adult Education, Manchester, on the 28th May, 1960, in the Playwrights' Workshop Festival by the Withington Players with the following cast of characters:

(in the order of their appearance)

MOTHER SUPERIOR	*Mollie K. Locke*
SISTER THÉRÈSE	*Florence Machin*
MARIE	*Jackie Lane*
MADAME LATTIER	*Joan Buckleton*

Produced by MOLLIE K. LOCKE, A.D.B.

The action of the Play takes place in the Mother Superior's room in a convent in northern France

Time—the Early 1950s

THE LULLABY

SCENE—*A room in a convent in France. It is a morning early in the 1950s. The room is sparsely furnished; there is a window C of the back wall, a door leading to the rest of the convent L and up R, against the R wall, is a bookcase full of books. There is a table C and above it, C, a chair. Upright chairs stand R and L of the window and below the bookcase R. On the table are letters, various papers, pen and ink, a small hand-bell, a pair of spectacles and a vase of flowers; in the table drawer is a small bone cross. On the wall R is a crucifix and one or two religious pictures may be added at the discretion of the producer.*

When the CURTAIN *rises the* MOTHER SUPERIOR *is seated at the table studying a letter. There is a knock at the door.*

MOTHER SUPERIOR. Come in!

(SISTER THÉRÈSE *enters, looking harassed*)

THÉRÈSE (*looking harassed*) Good morning, Mother, you sent for me?

MOTHER SUPERIOR (*smiling*) Good morning, Sister Thérèse, yes, I did. (*She sees Sister Thérèse's harassed expression*) But you seem upset. (*Gently*) Trouble with our young charges?

THÉRÈSE (*primly*) I thought at one time we were to have a mutiny on our hands, (*firmly*) but it is settled.

MOTHER SUPERIOR (*drily*) I heard various sounds from outside. Who was the culprit this time?

THÉRÈSE (*primly*) Michael.

MOTHER SUPERIOR (*in amused astonishment*) That angelic-looking child? And what has he been up to this time?

THÉRÈSE. The American tourists gave him some chewing-gum. After masticating it for days, he discovered it had certain other properties when applied to the girls' pigtails——

(*The* MOTHER SUPERIOR *looks at Sister Thérèse in amazement*)

—some of the girls have been washing their hair for days, trying to get the gum out.

MOTHER SUPERIOR (*sighing*) The march of progress. (*Musingly*) Chewing-gum? In my young days it was treacle. Did you punish him?

THÉRÈSE (*firmly*) I did. I put him on wood-gathering for a week. That should keep him busy with the amount of wood required for heating the girls' bath water.

MOTHER SUPERIOR (*thoughtfully*) The punishment fitting the crime . . .

THÉRÈSE (*firmly*) He's a wild boy. What he lacks in size he makes up for in mischief.

MOTHER SUPERIOR (*softly*) He's a boy—and like most of them here, he does not know what boyhood is. (*Sadly*) They've all been deprived of so much.

(*They both remain silent for a moment*)

(*Putting on a brisk air*) Now—the reason I asked you to see me. I am expecting a visitor. Six months ago I received a letter, (*she picks up the letter*) from a Madame Lattier, living in the town of Le Caillou—in Provence, (*slowly*) concerning her missing daughter . . .

THÉRÈSE (*sadly*) Another one?

(*The* MOTHER SUPERIOR *nods in reply*)

MOTHER SUPERIOR (*sadly*) She has been writing to the Mayor of every village in our district, asking for news of her missing child—a girl, taken from her in Ravensbruck concentration camp, when only three years old. The Mayor of our village wrote to her in answer that we had given sanctuary to a number of small children from Ravensbruck and other camps after the liberation.

THÉRÈSE (*thoughtfully*) A girl? From Ravensbruck? That means . . . ?

MOTHER SUPERIOR (*nodding*) Marie. (*She sighs*) In her letter Madame Lattier gave me all the details and a full description, (*thoughtfully*) and there is a possibility that the girl we know as Marie could be her daughter. At least, so far there is nothing to disprove it. (*She pauses*) Two days ago I received another letter, she has left Le Caillou and is on her way here—and will arrive today—soon.

THÉRÈSE (*in surprise*) Six months later? That does not sound like a devoted mother?

MOTHER SUPERIOR (*gently*) Who knows? It is not for us to judge.

THÉRÈSE (*musingly*) Eight years after—and still they search!

MOTHER SUPERIOR (*sadly*) Hope is something that never dies.

THÉRÈSE. I wasn't thinking only of that. Every time a parent visits us, searching for a son—or a daughter, (*with feeling*) everything is so upset. The children are not the same for weeks.

MOTHER SUPERIOR (*sadly*) The children also hope—and we are helpless.

THÉRÈSE (*warmly*) Nobody—nobody could have done more for the children than you have.

MOTHER SUPERIOR. If *one* child is left homeless, then we have failed.

THÉRÈSE (*feelingly*) I will not listen to such talk from you. After you have dedicated your life to the children.

MOTHER SUPERIOR (*smiling at Sister Thérèse*) And enjoyed every minute of it, (*accusingly*) and so have you though you try not to show it. (*Softly*) Memories can also be very precious.

THÉRÈSE (*gently*) Do not hurt yourself, you have done everything possible.

MOTHER SUPERIOR (*musingly*) Have I? I see an unwanted child—and I see parents—without children, searching vainly, and I feel that here could be a union that He would smile upon—and I can do nothing!

THÉRÈSE. That is not our fault. The authorities have given us strict instructions—proof of recognition between parents and child must be shown, or the matter is out of our hands.

MOTHER SUPERIOR (*sadly*) I know, but how does one tell that to a distraught mother or a sobbing child? (*Feelingly*)

The authorities tell us that there is always adoption—as if it were the final solution, but the would-be parents want the strong and healthy children. (*With a trace of bitterness*) Three times Armand has come up for adoption and three times they take one look at his twisted leg and pass on to another—and Sandra—(*slowly and with feeling*)—and Marie, (*she repeats it sadly*) and now, Marie—again . . .

    (SISTER THÉRÈSE *gestures in resignation. Both women remain silent with their thoughts for a few moments*)

(*Tonelessly*) I suppose we must go through it once more . . .
THÉRÈSE (*gently*) That is also out of our hands . . .
MOTHER SUPERIOR. True—true . . . (*She sighs*) So be it. I shall rely upon you to make our visitor welcome.
THÉRÈSE (*hurt*) All our visitors are made welcome.
MOTHER SUPERIOR (*gently*) I know, Sister, but this is something unusual—a peasant woman travelling five hundred miles across France on the slender hope of finding a daughter.
THÉRÈSE (*mollified*) I will attend to it. (*She turns to leave*)
MOTHER SUPERIOR (*smiling*) And, Sister Thérèse . . .

    (SISTER THÉRÈSE *stops*)

(*Smiling*) I suggest to keep Michael out of further mischief—tell cook to lock up the treacle.

    (SISTER THÉRÈSE *looks at the Mother Superior for a moment, then smiles warmly at her. The* MOTHER SUPERIOR *smiles back*)

We must not be too hard on our young delinquents.
THÉRÈSE (*ruefully*) That's the trouble. I couldn't be if I wanted to . . .
MOTHER SUPERIOR (*softly*) Bless you, Sister. I know that.
THÉRÈSE (*smiling in pleasure and stopping at the door*) I suppose you will wish to speak with Marie first?
MOTHER SUPERIOR (*thoughtfully*) I suppose so, I have not told her anything yet. Have her come in.

    (SISTER THÉRÈSE *nods and leaves. The* MOTHER SUPERIOR *picks up the letter again, absent-mindedly finding her spectacles*

THE LULLABY

amongst the pile of papers on her table, and putting them on, thoughtfully studies the letter again. A few moments later there is a knock at the door)

Come in!

(The door opens and MARIE *shyly enters and stands just inside the doorway. When she speaks carefully her speech, though slow, is clear and distinct. It is when she becomes excited and forgets that she stammers)*

MARIE *(speaking slowly and carefully as she has been taught; she curtsies)* Good morning, Mother Superior.

MOTHER SUPERIOR *(gently)* Good morning, Marie. *(She beckons Marie forward)* Come in, child.

*(*MARIE *comes shyly forward)*

(Trying to put Marie at her ease) I have heard excellent reports of your needlework, my child, and your teacher informs me you are making good progress in your studies.

MARIE *(slowly and distinctly)* Thank you—Mother Superior—I do—my best.

MOTHER SUPERIOR. I'm sure you do. Always remember, knowledge is a protection against the wickedness in the outside world. *(Sadly—half to herself)* We cannot prevent this wickedness but we can try to understand it. *(She pauses for a moment)* The doctor tells me your speech is much improved?

MARIE *(with obvious pleasure)* Oh—yes—Mother Superior.

MOTHER SUPERIOR *(gently probing)* And the nightmares?

MARIE *(her face clouding but still speaking cheerfully)* They do—not come—so often now . . .

MOTHER SUPERIOR *(sincerely)* Good! Good!—We'll soon remedy them altogether. *(She leans back at a loss as how to begin)* Now, Marie, there is a little matter I wish to discuss with you, *(she pauses)* about—the time when you first came to us, *(hesitatingly)* after—after you were found—we could not find any trace of your parents.

(At this point, MARIE *becomes a little upset. It shows in her speech for a short time)*

MARIE (*nervously*) I kn—kn—know—th—th—that—Mother Superior.
MOTHER SUPERIOR (*speaking slowly and carefully in an attempt to soothe Marie*) And from time to time, people come here searching for someone, a mother, a father—looking for a son or a daughter——
MARIE (*composing herself with an effort*) Yes, Mother, I've seen them.
MOTHER SUPERIOR. —and once in a while, only very occasionally, I'm afraid, they find the one they're looking for.
MARIE. Like—l—l—little—P—Paul? (*She speaks more slowly in an endeavour to speak more normally*) His—parents—took him—away . . .
MOTHER SUPERIOR. Yes, like Paul. (*She pauses for words*) Well, soon, later today . . .
MARIE (*impulsively interrupting*) Mother Superior, do you think the, (*in her excitement she has difficulty in speaking*) the l—l—lady—coming—t—today—w—*will*—be—my—m—mother?
MOTHER SUPERIOR (*looking at Marie in astonishment*) How did you know someone was coming?
MARIE (*flustered but speaking carefully once the initial excitement is over*) The girls and the boys, (*she pauses*) you see—we talk—about parents.
MOTHER SUPERIOR. But this was supposed to be a secret.
MARIE (*nervously*) Y—Yes—Mother Superior.
MOTHER SUPERIOR (*sighing*) Ah, well, the best laid plans . . . (*She pauses*) What do you talk about when you know a parent is coming?
MARIE (*forgetting her nervousness*) Oh, about having a proper home, a mother—a father—sisters and brothers . . .
MOTHER SUPERIOR (*wistfully*) Are you so unhappy here?
MARIE (*upset at the question; speaking vehemently but carefully*) Oh, Mother! It's not that! (*With a trace of sadness*) But at school the children from the village tell us of their homes, (*wistfully*) some of them have a whole bedroom to themselves. (*She looks at the Mother Superior with love*) We all know how kind you and the others are—but . . . (*She becomes lost for words*)

MOTHER SUPERIOR (*sadly, half to herself*) But! (*She sighs*) I understand, child. (*She gathers Marie to her in a tender embrace*)

(MARIE *cries and buries her head in the Mother Superior's shoulder*)

There—there! (*She gently strokes Marie's head*) Don't cry, child. You know what you've been taught? For everything He does there is a reason.

MARIE (*lifting her head and slowly returning to normal*) Yes, Mother Superior.

MOTHER SUPERIOR (*briskly*) Since you already know all about it, I shall not waste too much time. A lady *is* coming today. She thinks—you may be her daughter.

MARIE (*firmly*) She *will* be my mother—I know it!

MOTHER SUPERIOR (*gently*) Don't set your hopes too high, my child. More often, it is not so.

MARIE (*again having difficulty in speaking*) Sh—she—is—my —m—mother . . .

MOTHER SUPERIOR (*sighing as she watches* MARIE) I hope so—I hope so, but in case she is not . . . (*She sees Marie is beginning to show signs of tears again and stops*) Go now and make yourself ready, (*she smiles*) if she is your mother we can't having you looking like one of the scarecrows in the vineyards—can we?

MARIE (*half-smiling through the tears*) No, Mother Superior.

MOTHER SUPERIOR (*smiling back*) That's better. Now run along, child.

(MARIE *leaves. A few seconds elapse. The* MOTHER SUPERIOR, *lost in thought, shakes her head as if mentally deciding something. There is a knock at the door*)

(*Looking up*) Come in!

(*The door opens and* SISTER THÉRÈSE *enters and comes over to the Mother Superior*)

THÉRÈSE. Well?
MOTHER SUPERIOR (*smiling*) Well what?
THÉRÈSE (*impatiently*) What did Marie say?
MOTHER SUPERIOR (*gently*) Oh, she was most helpful, she

told me all about the expected arrival of her mother.
THÉRÈSE (*her mouth opening in astonishment*) She what?
MOTHER SUPERIOR (*amused*) She knows more about it than I do. (*She shrugs*) Marie knows the arrival is her mother.
THÉRÈSE (*still bewildered*) She knows?

(*The* MOTHER SUPERIOR *nods her head amusedly in answer. The two women look at each other for a moment then laugh*)

MOTHER SUPERIOR (*after a few moments*) The child is much better, (*she pauses*) but I am frightened . . .
THÉRÈSE (*gently*) In case the woman is not her mother?
MOTHER SUPERIOR (*first nodding in answer to Sister Thérèse's question*) Another hurt may undo the work of years.
THÉRÈSE. I agree. (*She reminds herself*) Oh, I forgot, the mother, (*she catches herself in vexation*) I mean Madame Lattier has arrived.
MOTHER SUPERIOR. I know.
THÉRÈSE (*in mild, astonished disgust*) Everybody knows everything around here, except me. You must have seen her from the window?
MOTHER SUPERIOR (*smiling*) No, I heard the children scampering down the hall in excitement to see something. (*Drily*) If the children can put two and two together, then surely we are not too old to learn from them?

(SISTER THÉRÈSE *shakes her head in resignation*)

What type of woman is our visitor?
THÉRÈSE (*shrugging*) A woman! A peasant! (*Gently*) With sorrow in her eyes.
MOTHER SUPERIOR (*softly*) A description that fits so many people in these troubled times. Have you shown Madame to her room?
THÉRÈSE. I offered to, (*gently*) but I think she would rather see you first before anything. (*She shakes her head sadly*) She is waiting outside as if each moment was an eternity.
MOTHER SUPERIOR (*sighing in sad resignation*) Bring her in.
THÉRÈSE. Yes, Mother.

(SISTER THÉRÈSE *leaves the room. The* MOTHER SUPERIOR

looks upward in prayer, then clasping her hands and gazing out of the window, waits patiently and motionlessly.
A few moments pass and the door opens. SISTER THÉRÈSE *enters with* MADAME LATTIER *who is carrying a travelling bag*)

THÉRÈSE. Mother Superior—Madame Lattier.

(MADAME LATTIER *bows*)

MOTHER SUPERIOR. Welcome to the Convent of Notre Dame, Madame Lattier.

LATTIER. Thank you, Reverend Mother.

MOTHER SUPERIOR (*to Sister Thérèse*) A chair for our guest, please.

(SISTER THÉRÈSE *brings the chair* L *of the window for Madame Lattier to* L *of the table.* MADAME LATTIER *sits down, putting the travelling bag at her feet.* SISTER THÉRÈSE *stands by watching*)

I trust you had a pleasant journey?

LATTIER. I saw many things that were not pleasant.

MOTHER SUPERIOR (*sighing*) I'm afraid our country still bears the scars of war.

LATTIER (*sadly*) And the people.

MOTHER SUPERIOR. True—true. (*To Sister Thérèse*) See that Marie is ready but do not bring her in until I ring.

THÉRÈSE. Yes, Mother Superior.

(SISTER THÉRÈSE *goes out*)

LATTIER. Marie?

MOTHER SUPERIOR. The name we gave the girl we found. (*She pauses*) Your daughter's name was . . . ?

LATTIER. Madeleine.

MOTHER SUPERIOR. Yes, of course, so you stated in your letter, (*she pauses and picks up the letter*) which I have read most carefully, madame, and also investigated the facts and information you supplied, (*she pauses again*) and I must admit there is a possibility that the girl, Marie—taken from Ravensbruck concentration camp eight years ago—may be your daughter . . .

(MADAME LATTIER *regards the Mother Superior impassively*)

The times and dates you gave us coincide with those we have. Your description of your child fits that of Marie—but obviously this description could also apply to many of the female children taken from the camps. Did your daughter have any identification marks?

LATTIER (*with a little pride*) No, she was a perfect baby.

MOTHER SUPERIOR (*sighing*) Perhaps so, but it makes our task all the more difficult. You see, without anything conclusive we must rely upon some form of recognition between parent and child.

LATTIER (*firmly*) I shall know my own daughter.

MOTHER SUPERIOR (*with emphasis*) Madame Lattier! I assure you, that after eight years it is extremely difficult. In your mind you have the remembrance of your child, but that child is now a girl or a young woman—and as difficult as it is for a parent to recognize a child after all this time, it is almost impossible for the child to remember anything. (*She pauses*) I must warn you—many come in hope—and return in despair!

LATTIER (*moved by the Mother Superior's sincerity*) I understand.

MOTHER SUPERIOR. We do all we can, but our instructions from the authorities are very clear on one point, (*with emphasis*) there must be some indication shown that the child is yours!

(MADAME LATTIER *nods in understanding*)

And without proof we are instructed *not* to release a child, (*with feeling*) as much as we would like to do at times. (*Gently*) We have to be strict, but it is not of our own choosing.

LATTIER (*becoming a little more friendly*) What becomes of the children who are not claimed?

MOTHER SUPERIOR (*sadly*) We do our best, and try to find them good homes with foster-parents. Unfortunately most people have their own problems—and we have to be careful. We want the children to have an opportunity in life, happiness and love, to try to forget what they have suffered. (*She pauses*) Obviously, only so many are lucky in finding such a home. (*She looks directly at Madame Lattier*) And those are usually the ones who do not show too much of the suffering they have endured...

LATTIER. I do not understand.

MOTHER SUPERIOR (*carefully*) We have many children under this roof—(*gently*) and not all are well...

(MADAME LATTIER *tenses and leans forward*)

Many show some effect of the tragedy they have experienced.

LATTIER (*clasping her hands together in agitation*) Madeleine—Marie?

MOTHER SUPERIOR (*gently*) She was not as bad as some when she came here. She was, (*she pauses while she searches for the correct words*) nervous—it affected her speech and movement—for two years she could only say an odd word...

LATTIER (*with feeling*) And now?

MOTHER SUPERIOR. Almost well. Her movements are normal and her affliction of speech is fast disappearing, it only shows when she is nervous or excited, but the doctors say that this is common to many people, who have not been through what this child has.

(MADAME LATTIER *bends her head in relief*)

The child still has the occasional nightmare and we do what we can, (*sadly*) but whatever we do for the children in our care, we cannot give them the individual love and affection that only parents can give.

LATTIER (*simply*) I am sure of one thing, Reverend Mother, the children in your care are most fortunate.

MOTHER SUPERIOR (*sadly*) We do what we can, but it is like a drop in the ocean.

(*Both women remain silent for a moment*)

LATTIER (*nervously*) You spoke of giving the children opportunity. If the girl *is* my daughter, I am a poor woman.

MOTHER SUPERIOR (*simply*) If the child finds happiness with you—nothing else matters—*that* is *her* opportunity!

(*There is a short pause*)

(*Gently*) Now, there are a few questions I must ask.
LATTIER. I understand.
MOTHER SUPERIOR (*taking pen and paper*) The father?
LATTIER (*impassively*) Dead! In Auschwitz!
MOTHER SUPERIOR (*softly*) I'm sorry . . .
LATTIER (*feeling in her bag*) I have the marriage certificate. (*She finds the certificate and hands it to the Mother Superior*)
MOTHER SUPERIOR (*first glancing at the certificate*) Where was your daughter born?
LATTIER. Le Caillou, Provence. (*She brings out a second certificate and hands it to the Mother Superior*)
MOTHER SUPERIOR (*putting on her spectacles and studying the second certificate*) Hum, female child, (*she writes the particulars down as she reads*) Madeleine Nicolle, father—Pierre Lattier—mother—Mathilde. (*She pauses*) Have you any other children?

(MADAME LATTIER *shakes her head*)

(*Deciding*) Well, I think we have sufficient details, (*she leans back*) but before I have the child brought in—what do you intend to do? As I explained to you, by law, we must have some indication of relationship.
LATTIER (*impassively*) I shall know my own daughter.
MOTHER SUPERIOR (*gently*) But that is not proof to us.
LATTIER. I have brought her doll. (*She feels in the bag and brings out an old, tattered doll. She looks at the doll and speaks tenderly*) She was so fond of it. And there was a game we played with sweets, she had to guess how many were held in the closed hand and she was given them, and the only number she could say was four, (*musingly*) always she said four . . .
MOTHER SUPERIOR (*gently probing*) Anything else?
LATTIER. The lullaby.
MOTHER SUPERIOR. Ah, yes, the lullaby—you mentioned it in your letter.
LATTIER. It is an old folk-song of our district. (*Brokenly*) She was so frightened in the camp and could not sleep. I used to sing it to her and she would fall asleep in my arms. (*She breaks down and weeps*)
MOTHER SUPERIOR (*softly*) I understand. (*She waits a*

few moments and then speaks with sympathy) Compose yourself, madame, and we will have the child brought in, (*she speaks with gentle urgency*) and please, try not to upset her too much.

(MADAME LATTIER *dries her tears. The* MOTHER SUPERIOR *rings a little hand-bell.*
The door opens and SISTER THÉRÈSE *enters. She looks inquiringly at the Mother Superior*)

Where is Marie, now?
THÉRÈSE. In the dormitory—waiting.
MOTHER SUPERIOR. Please fetch her.
THÉRÈSE. Yes, Mother.

(SISTER THÉRÈSE *leaves the room. The* MOTHER SUPERIOR *and* MADAME LATTIER *relax and wait for Marie*)

MOTHER SUPERIOR (*musingly*) There is one thing I do not understand. You first wrote to me six months ago, yet you arrive only now?
LATTIER (*impassively*) I had to save for my fare—and one other. My wages are small.
MOTHER SUPERIOR (*in surprise*) There are funds for this purpose.
LATTIER (*impassively*) I do not ask for charity.
MOTHER SUPERIOR (*nodding in appreciation of Madame Lattier's principles*) What work do you do?
LATTIER. Whatever I can get. In the season I pick grapes in the vineyards, or work as a maid—or scrub floors . . .
MOTHER SUPERIOR (*with feeling*) All that to obtain money for a fare—to see a child you may not even know? (*She pauses*) And if she is not your daughter?
LATTIER (*impassively*) I scrub more floors—pick more grapes—and search again.
MOTHER SUPERIOR (*softly*) How many times have you made this journey?
LATTIER (*tonelessly*) This is the fifth time in seven years.
MOTHER SUPERIOR (*shocked*) Mother of God!

(MADAME LATTIER *looks expectantly at the door*)

(*Not yet recovered from her amazement she sees the look*) They will be here soon, the dormitory is in the other wing.

(*They both remain silent for a few moments, waiting. Then* MADAME LATTIER *commences to speak. She speaks half to herself as if unburdening her soul*)

LATTIER (*commencing in a monotonous, impassive tone*) They told me I could not bear a child. I would die! For ten years my husband and myself endured a childless marriage. (*With feeling*) In ten years he never uttered a word of reproach, (*with passion*) until I decided that a woman without child might as well be dead anyway. I was a middle-aged woman when Madeleine was born to me, and I should have died in giving birth, but God was good, and I was spared, and I was the mother of the loveliest child I could hope for, (*softly with gentle pleasure*) for three years—three happy years, (*tonelessly again*) and now I must find her, or I am as nothing!

MOTHER SUPERIOR (*softly*) May He reward your search!

(*They both remain silent. There is a knock at the door.* MADAME LATTIER *tenses*)

Come in!

(*The door opens and* SISTER THÉRÈSE *enters with* MARIE *who has put on her best clothes. She now wears steel-rimmed spectacles and she has put a coloured ribbon in her hair. She clutches Sister Thérèse's robe in nervousness*)

(*Gently*) Do not be afraid, my child, no harm will come to you.

(MADAME LATTIER, *her face showing emotion, rises and stands staring at* MARIE, *who still nervously clutches Sister Thérèse's robe*)

(*Soothingly to Marie*) Marie, this lady is Madame Lattier.

(MARIE *does not answer*)

(*She speaks in a firmer tone*) Marie, remember your manners!

(MARIE *comes nervously out from Sister Thérèse's robe and nervously curtsies to Madame Lattier.* MADAME LATTIER, *oblivious of everybody except Marie, goes over to her and places her hands gently on Marie's shoulders and looks searchingly into her face*)

LATTIER (*softly; to herself*) It could be, it could be!

(MARIE *remains motionless*)

(*Gently*) Do you recognize me, Madeleine?

(MARIE *looks nervously at the Mother Superior*)

MOTHER SUPERIOR (*gently*) That was the name of Madame Lattier's daughter.

LATTIER (*with a little feeling*) Do you recognize me?

MOTHER SUPERIOR (*gently*) Give her time, she is still a child. (*To Marie*) My dear, this lady may be your mother. Do you remember anything?

(MARIE *shakes her head*)

LATTIER (*picking up the doll*) Don't you remember your doll? You played with it for hours. (*She pushes the doll into Marie's hands*)

(MARIE *looks down at it uncomprehendingly*)

(*With increased feeling*) Do you remember it?

(MARIE *slowly and nervously shakes her head.* MADAME LATTIER *looks beseechingly at the Mother Superior.* SISTER THÉRÈSE *takes the doll out of Marie's unresisting hands and places it on a chair. The* MOTHER SUPERIOR *looks silently back at Madame Lattier*)

(*Humbly to the Mother Superior*) I do not know.

MOTHER SUPERIOR (*gently*) Try again.

(MADAME LATTIER *turns to Marie and holds up her clenched hand*)

LATTIER. Do you remember this game? How many sweets are in my hand?

(MARIE *looks to the Mother Superior and Sister Thérèse for guidance. They look back at her sadly*)

MOTHER SUPERIOR (*to Marie; gently*) Try.

MARIE (*to Madame Lattier*) I don't—know . . .

MOTHER SUPERIOR (*gently to Marie*) I realize it is eight

years since you saw your mother and it is very difficult—but do your best. Do you remember anything?

MARIE (*slowly and sadly*) No—Mother—Superior . . .

MOTHER SUPERIOR. If this lady is your mother, do you want to go with her?

(MARIE *nervously but decidedly nods her head*)

LATTIER (*brokenly*) But she does not remember anything.

THÉRÈSE. Give the child time.

LATTIER (*sadly*) It is no use.

MOTHER SUPERIOR (*sighing*) It is never easy. Try again.

(MADAME LATTIER *visibly composes herself and gently takes hold of Marie's arms.* MARIE *looks up at her trustingly*)

LATTIER. Do you remember Annette?

(*The name has a pronounced effect on* MARIE. *At first her brow furrows in thought and concentration as her mind searches back through the dim past*)

MARIE (*half to herself*) Annette? Annette! (*Her face goes blank*) Annette . . .

LATTIER (*frightened*) She is remembering . . .

MARIE (*now oblivious of her surroundings, she shows extreme fright. She speaks perfectly without any difficulty*) Don't hit me, please! (*She is in another world*) The fires! (*She becomes hysterical*) The smoke! They're burning!

(SISTER THÉRÈSE *quickly gathers the girl to her and comforts her*)

MOTHER SUPERIOR (*urgently; to Sister Thérèse*) Take her outside until I call you!

THÉRÈSE (*to Marie—gently stroking her head*) Now, child, you know Sister Thérèse—don't cry . . .

(SISTER THÉRÈSE *gently escorts* MARIE *out of the room*)

LATTIER (*in distress*) The poor child!

(*The* MOTHER SUPERIOR *does not answer but sadly shakes her head*)

(*Sitting wearily down and repeating to herself*) The poor child!

MOTHER SUPERIOR. Madame, please listen to me, it may be important.

(MADAME LATTIER *lifts her head and dully regards the Mother Superior*)

(*Steadily*) Who was Annette?

LATTIER (*dully*) A girl—about the same age as my Madeleine. Her father was also dead and her mother died soon after they arrived at the camp. The two girls played together—so I looked after her—until—we—were separated . . .

MOTHER SUPERIOR (*thoughtfully*) The two children were together for some months?

(MADAME LATTIER *nods disinterestedly in answer*)

(*After concentrating for a moment*) Madame, please compose yourself, and listen carefully to what I have to say.

(*The tone of the Mother Superior's voice causes* MADAME LATTIER *to sit up with a little interest*)

When you last saw your child, did she have any personal possessions?

LATTIER. No, they took everything of value away from both of us. All we had were the few rags we were wearing.

MOTHER SUPERIOR. All the clothes were burnt by the liberation authorities. She had nothing?

LATTIER. No. (*She concentrates*) One moment. She *did* have one possession . . . After we had arrived at the camp, one of the other prisoners gave her something—(*slowly remembering*) a cross—a little one, about three inches long. (*Bitterly*) The Boches placed no value on it.

MOTHER SUPERIOR (*showing a little excitement*) Can you describe this cross. What was it made of?

LATTIER (*concentrating*) Like bone—I think it was from an old knife-handle.

(*They both remain lost in thought for a few moments with the* MOTHER SUPERIOR *obviously trying to decide something. Finally the* MOTHER SUPERIOR, *as if making up her mind, goes over to the window, looks out and then returning to the table, takes a small object out of the table-drawer and coming over to Madame Lattier, places her hand gently on her shoulder*)

MOTHER SUPERIOR (*softly*) Madame, I have something to tell you.

(MADAME LATTIER *looks up at the Mother Superior*)

Marie was brought to us with another girl about the same age. The other girl was very ill. (*Gently and sorrowfully*) She died soon after she arrived here . . .

(MADAME LATTIER, *showing emotion, tenses in the chair as she gazes at the Mother Superior*)

One of the girls was clutching, (*she pauses and opens her hand, showing Madame Lattier the object she is holding*) a—small—bone—cross!

LATTIER (*looking at the cross*) That was—my daughter's!

(*The* MOTHER SUPERIOR *looks down sadly*)

(*Steeling herself and finding difficulty in speaking*) Which—girl—had—the cross?

MOTHER SUPERIOR (*gently*) You wish me to answer?

(MADAME LATTIER *nods dully*)

(*Speaking quickly to hide her emotion*) We took it from the hand of the dead girl.

(MADAME LATTIER *bends her head in anguish for a moment, then makes the sign of the cross*)

LATTIER (*dully*) It is strange but I have no more tears.

MOTHER SUPERIOR. In all fairness, there is something I must tell you. The fact that the cross came off the dead girl—does not necessarily mean it belonged to her . . .

(MADAME LATTIER *stares at the Mother Superior in bewilderment*)

In all the confusion and chaos at that time, nobody could be certain of anything. In the disorder the children could have picked up the first thing that came to hand. Half of them did not even know their own names.

THE LULLABY

LATTIER (*hopelessly*) It means nothing. I know now my daughter is dead.

MOTHER SUPERIOR. After eight years we cannot be sure of anything. We have tried to unite families wherever possible, but who can speak with certainty? (*Steadily*) We do know one thing. Marie is alive and needs a mother's love and care!

LATTIER (*for the moment—not understanding*) But she is not . . . (*Her voice dies away and she looks at the Mother Superior*)

(*The MOTHER SUPERIOR returns her look steadily. There is a few moments pause*)

(*Gently*) I understand.

MOTHER SUPERIOR. There is still the lullaby.

(MADAME LATTIER *shakes her head in indecision*)

(*Gently*) Will you try?

LATTIER. She will have to be told.

MOTHER SUPERIOR. Yes, she will—but that can come later.

(MADAME LATTIER *bends her head in thought for a moment, then lifts it and nods to the Mother Superior. The* MOTHER SUPERIOR *smiles thankfully and rings the hand-bell. The door opens and* SISTER THÉRÈSE *enters*)

Bring the child in.

(SISTER THÉRÈSE *exits for a second. She returns with a more composed* MARIE)

(*Kindly to Marie*) Do not be afraid, Marie. We are not going to ask you any more questions. (*She pauses*) We just want to know if this song means anything to you.

(MARIE *remains motionless next to Sister Thérèse. The* MOTHER SUPERIOR *looks towards* MADAME LATTIER *who, first bending her head as if in silent prayer, commences to sing the lullaby without lifting her head, almost as if she is afraid to look at Marie. She continues to sing alone for a few seconds, while* MARIE *listens with obvious growing attention, then slowly and with much concentration, joining in. They sing together for a few seconds until the* MOTHER SUPERIOR *signals to* MADAME LATTIER *to stop.* MARIE *continues to sing alone for a few moments until realizing she is singing by herself, stops in confusion. There is a significant pause*)

THÉRÈSE (*in an awed tone*) Mercy be!

(MARIE, *with a little of her memory returning, cries*)

LATTIER (*first looking at the Mother Superior in understanding, holds her arms out to Marie*) My child!

(MARIE *remains motionless for a moment.* SISTER THÉRÈSE *gives a gentle push and* MARIE *runs sobbing into Madame Lattier's arms*)

MARIE. Mother!

LATTIER (*repeating the word in stunned delight*) Mother!

(*The* MOTHER SUPERIOR *and* SISTER THÉRÈSE *look on for a few moments*)

MOTHER SUPERIOR (*speaking briskly to cover her emotion*) Now—we have much to do. Papers, certificates, affidavits for proof of recognition, (*she speaks gently to Madame Lattier*) but it has been enough for one day, (*with gentle feeling*) and I imagine you would like to be alone with your—daughter?

LATTIER (*to Mother Superior*) May God bless you! (*She picks up the little cross*) May I keep this—for a remembrance?

(*The* MOTHER SUPERIOR *nods*)

(*With emotion*) And I would like to say a prayer—over—the—other girl's—grave . . .

(*The* MOTHER SUPERIOR *nods in understanding*)

MOTHER SUPERIOR (*softly*) Now go with your child.

(MADAME LATTIER *looks at Marie with love, then holds her hand out.*

MARIE *takes it with complete trust and they walk out together, oblivious of all except each other. The* MOTHER SUPERIOR *and* SISTER THÉRÈSE *remain silent.* SISTER THÉRÈSE *automatically picks up the doll and returns it to the bag, then puts the bag away neatly in a corner. The* MOTHER

Superior *absent-mindedly picks up the letter, looks at it without seeing it and puts it back on the table, then goes over to the window and looks out.* Sister Thérèse *joins her*)

Thérèse (*looking out and dabbing a furtive tear*) Look at them! After eight years they have found each other! (*Feelingly*) They will bring each other much happiness . . .

Mother Superior. There is so little of it in the world today.

Thérèse. The wheels grind slowly—but . . .

Mother Superior (*gently interrupting*) *But* sometimes they require a little aid.

Thérèse (*in surprise*) Ah?

Mother Superior (*musingly*) Yes, they *will* bring each other much happiness . . .

Thérèse (*still surprised*) That's what I said.

Mother Superior. But Marie is *not* her daughter . . .

Thérèse (*shocked*) What are you saying?

Mother Superior. The child is not Madame Lattier's daughter.

Thérèse (*in disbelief*) But you heard—the lullaby . . . ?

Mother Superior. There was one other person who would remember the lullaby. Both Madame Lattier and I knew it.

(Sister Thérèse *looks at the Mother Superior in bafflement*)

An orphan child Madame Lattier cared for in the camp with her own child.

Thérèse (*understanding*) Then Marie is——?

Mother Superior. —Annette. (*She looks out of the window again*) But there goes one child who will find some of the happiness she has so long been deprived of.

(*They both stand and stare out of the window*)

(*Half to herself*) I hope I have done the right thing . . .

In answer Sister Thérèse *puts her hand gently on the* Mother Superior's *arm. They both continue to gaze out of the window as—*

the Curtain *falls*

FURNITURE AND PROPERTY PLOT

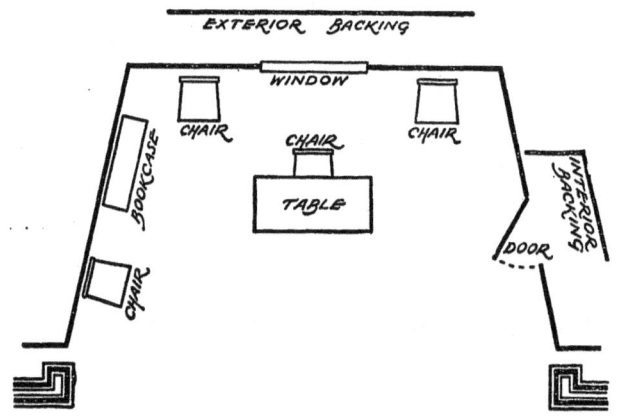

On stage: Wooden table. *On it:* letters, papers, pen and ink, small hand-bell, spectacles, vase of flowers. *In table drawer:* small bone cross

4 upright chairs

Bookcase. *In it:* books

Crucifix

Religious pictures

Curtains at window

Off stage: Travelling bag. *In it:* an old doll, 2 certificates (MADAME LATTIER)

LIGHTING PLOT

No property fittings required

Interior. The same scene throughout

THE APPARENT SOURCE OF LIGHT is a window C of the back wall

THE MAIN ACTING AREAS are C, RC and LC

To open: Effect of morning sunlight

No cues

EFFECTS PLOT

Cue 1	At the rise of the CURTAIN	(Page 1)
	Knock at the door	
Cue 2	MOTHER SUPERIOR studies the letter	(Page 5)
	Knock at the door	
Cue 3	MARIE leaves. THE MOTHER SUPERIOR stands lost in thought	(Page 7)
	Knock at the door	
Cue 4	MOTHER SUPERIOR: ". . . reward your search!"	(Page 14)
	Knock at the door	

www.ingramcontent.com/pod-product-compliance
Lightning Source LLC
Chambersburg PA
CBHW070456050426
42450CB00012B/3297